Beasts of Eden

Beasts of Eden

Poems

Michael Beadle

Press 53
Winston-Salem

Press 53, LLC
PO Box 30314
Winston-Salem, NC 27130

First Edition

Copyright © 2018 by Michael Beadle

All rights reserved, including the right of reproduction in whole or in part in any form except in the case of brief quotations embodied in critical articles or reviews. For permission, contact publisher at editor@Press53.com, or at the address above.

Cover design by Kevin Morgan Watson

Cover art, "Beasts of Eden," Copyright © 2018
by Dawn Surratt, used by permission of the artist.
instagram.com/ddhanna

Author photo by André Bassett

Library of Congress Control Number
2018938184

Printed on acid-free paper
ISBN 978-1-941209-80-6

In memory of
Kathryn Stripling Byer
and
Susan Laughter Meyers

The author thanks the editors of the journals where these poems first appeared:

Great Smokies Review: "Girl with Guitar, 1947"

Invitation (Main Street Rag): "In God We rust"

Kakalak: "Yay-long," "Milk and Honey" (as "Enough Already"), and "Alex"

Main Street Rag: "Alive"

Nazim Hikmet Poetry Festival: a chapbook of talks and poetry: "David"

The New Southerner: "Out of Season"

Redheaded Stepchild: "Fallen" (as "Falling")

The Southern Poetry Anthology, Vol. VII: North Carolina: "Spearfinger"

Sow's Ear: "Silas Morgan's Collection"

Wild Goose Creek Review: "Flesh and Blood," "Sisyphus in the Parking Lot," and "Trace"

www.ncarts.org: "The Naming," "Shibboleth," and "Silent Night"

Contents

I.
The Naming	3
Silas Morgan's Collection	4
Fallen	5
Silent Night	6
The Loving Tree	7
Last Embrace	8
The Schoolhouse	9
The Letter	10
Out of Season	12
The Butterfly	13
Wild Horses	15
Alex	16
Alive	18

II.
Shibboleth	21
Yay-long	22
Toothjumping	23
Shine	24
The Flood	25
The Devil Beats His Wife	26
Flesh and Blood	27
Bull Elk in Cataloochee	28
Girl with Guitar, 1947	29
Infare, 1898	31
Home Guard	33

III.
Spearfinger	37
Uk'tena	39
Beasts of Eden	40
David	41
Milk and Honey	42
Samson	43
In God We rust	44
Sisyphus in the Parking Lot	45

The Golden Cup	47
Pills for Pygmalion	48
Trace	49
Mad Scientist	50
Superman's Laundry	51
Problems with Flight	52
Endnotes	55
Acknowledgments	57
Author Biography	59
Cover Artist Biography	61

I.

Into the darkness they go, the wise and lovely.

— Edna St. Vincent Millay

The Naming

"What about this one?" I asked.
"Mylax," he replied.
"And this one?"
"Plumdrum."

We were at the lakeshore again
among the cool bed of rocks,
our words echoing
across the water.

Ghozlak   Aya   Zephanos

Lifting each rock,
we felt its weight in our palms,
closed our eyes
until a name arose.

Millanthium   Whillet   Lippery

We hurled the rocks
as far as we could
into the lake, giving them
a new depth to find.

There we sat for hours,
the only ones left in this world
who could conjure
its litany of names.

Perio   Shezai   Calex

As darkness crept into the cove,
we chose new rocks,
hardened by time, tempered by water,
and steadied our minds
for the Naming.

Silas Morgan's Collection

He keeps them at his gas station,
in dozens of Mason jars,
the biggest ones in paint buckets.
When work is slow, I stop by
for a Coke and conversation.
The universe keeps falling apart,
he says. *Some folks just lucky to find
the pieces.* He grins behind
a bushy beard, his seasoned hands
unwrapping a rag to reveal
the latest load from Sugar Cove—
clumps of mangled screws and rusty lugnuts,
gobs of melted washers, plunky
fishing weights, parts torn from old engines.
When I walk home, the stars
are full of sky. Lucky Silas,
holding his bits of heaven
before the junkyard takes us all away.

Fallen

It comes in the middle of the night
just when you realize you forgot
to lock the back door.

Glass shatters and you recall
sandlot games when a home run meant
hiding in the bushes.

Flick the bathroom light, find a hole.
Broken tiles, a strange rock.
You want to pick it up, but
TV has taught you to treat it
like a crime scene.
Better call the authorities.

No doubt, they'll carry it away
to some undisclosed lab, study
what we're not supposed to know.

Neighbors in bathrobes scan their lawns
with metal detector eyes, eager to seize
a little tabloid fame, secretly wish
such things would fall
into their homes.

They ask if you saw UFO lights.
You want to say *yes*.
Maybe you will. Or maybe
you remember that piece of you
fallen into someone else's life—
so sudden, so dangerous,
it had to be taken away.

Silent Night

flakes feather-fall
everything soft as a prayer

blurry streetlamps
an eerie lemon

deserted pick-up
wipers caught in mid-sweep

inches rise
clouds mound

your face aglow
in kitchen candlelight

a burn on my lips
as I kiss your forehead

twice
for good luck

not wanting
to break the spell

of a night that made us
mute with wonder

not wanting
to say anything

wanting the snow
to say it for me

The Loving Tree

Where are you now, Katy and Corey?
Did you make it through the summer of '87
when you notched your names
on this beech beside the creek?

What about you, J + P?
Are you living in a cul-de-sac with
a couple of kids and a black lab?
Or did you settle down on a farm
to raise chickens and a herd of cattle?
Do you ever get the urge to return
to this trail, trace the curves
of a mango-shaped heart where
only your initials fit inside?

So many letters. It's hard to know
where one couple ends and another begins.
Isn't that the ultimate equation:
everyone added up?

Will you, Ali, still take Chris
long after this etching fades?
Does love burn stronger when carved
with the sharpest of knives?

Do you regret, KT & DG,
this place that bears the scars
of sworn promises?

Do you ever worry some fool
might gash this sacred trunk,
add n to ever, X over
the arrow of Eros?

For what is love
but an open wound
for the ants to inspect?

Last Embrace

Dozers unearth the remains
of a couple buried near Verona.

Townsfolk gather to gossip.
Double suicide or ritual murder?

PhDs peruse the bony clues.
Note how the skulls face each other,

defying burial, teeth still intact.
What drove these neolithic lovers

to an early grave? No lips to hide
their petrified grins. What words

do we have for their mouths?
Something ate at their insides.

Ribs went missing. Femurs stack
so close in fetal pose, it's hard to know

whose limb is whose and why
frozen fingers still clutch a jaw

for that final kiss.

The Schoolhouse

We found it abandoned in the woods,
creaked inside. Along clapboard we knelt
among toppled shelves and the slow decay
of rotting books, a forest reclaiming its dead.
Vines climbed through loose floorboards.
Sawbriar strangled seatless chairs.
What bound us to these moth-bitten words of
Dante and Dickens, Jane Eyre and Huck Finn,
War and Peace? What summoned us
to these verses of Ovid and Homer,
Sappho and Cicero, Virgil and Sophocles?
When strangers came to plunder this library,
did they find themselves captives,
chalking the walls with their curséd names?
Or did they escape through a hole of pale light
where sky pierced roof and stars learned to read
what man once knew of myth and history?
How long did we rest by that stone fireplace,
studying the scattered pages of ageless stories,
content with a mystery that lingers
and a heart that never tires of learning?

The Letter

You gave it to me
before leaving, but I

stowed it away
for safe keeping,

waited for
the right hour

to read it.
Days turned cold.

I awoke one morning
alone and afraid,

wanting to read
your words,

wanting to trace
the looping lines

you spent on me.
In the ruins

of an old house
we once shared,

I rummaged through
trunks and closets,

pages and boxes.
Some days I find it—

pieces stuffed
in a drawer,

under stacks of receipts,
in the pocket

of an old shirt
I haven't worn in years—

crumpled sheets,
torn sentences

I straighten
and tape together,

this endless letter
I will never finish reading.

Out of Season

Plump as beachballs,
hollowed by sticky spoons,
a row of glowing heads

grinning missing teeth
lined the backyard walkway
for our feast of the dead.

When day broke, the spell lifted.
Tea light candles dried up,
but the heads remained. Each face

melted like a wicked witch.
Squinty eyes and crooked noses
withered into worm candy

until even the ants ignored them.
Under moonlight, they bleached into
paperskin crusts of their former selves,

ghostly footprints lost in snow.
Now the mower sputters passing over
those spots where the grass won't grow.

The Butterfly

I could not tell you.
My voice had forgotten the words.

I could not sing it to you.
The notes hung dry in my mouth.

So I had to wait for you
to find me in the woodshed.

Mourning cloak they call me,
Nymphalis antiopa,

a delicate thing with dark stained wings,
the color of worn leather, my edges

streaked yellow, dotted blue,
as if hurriedly painted.

Under thin light of dawn
you carried me inside.

How could I tell you what I was,
reborn from another life?

Once a proud wife,
I wanted nothing,

but the man I married
became the father I'd fled:

snarling brute, beer in hand,
looking for a body to test his rage.

I learned to hide,
run when I had to,

but he knew I'd come back,
to give him another chance.

One night, I sought release,
plunged into a lake

in a dress sewn with stones,
only to wake in the soon-after

hungry for willow leaves
and the sweet taste of elm and aspen.

All summer I flew, sucking oak sap
and nectar, trying to find a sturdy barn

where I could rest. When you
brought me in from the cold,

the warmth of a fire
startled my wings.

I wouldn't last long.
I only hope your love

will carry me
into a better world.

Wild Horses

They know they'll never stand again—
the bay colt missing a hind leg,
the palomino whose front hoof

came unglued, the cream-coated filly
with ebony ears and a clipped tail.
Porcelain stallions paraded for decades

on living room doilies, unbridled mares
guarding crystal jars of peppermints.
Silent companions of cocktail parties,

Christmas dinners, afternoon tea.
If Oma gave them names, I never knew.
After she died, they spent months

wrapped in newspaper,
boxed on basement shelves.
Perhaps they grew restless,

kicked each other in a barn-fire panic,
hoping to free themselves for the rainy day
when strangers came to haggle over

the china I'd never use. Let them
take the pewter goblets, the steins that smelled
like old pencils, tubs of tools

that bore the scars of hard seasons.
The tray of horses was all I hoped to keep.
I came to love them—

not for what they once were,
but, being broken,
how they went on living.

Alex

He hangs on the wall of your TV room:
a soldier not yet twenty, stiff and sober
in his Polish Army uniform.

Wool suit, black boots, shiny buttons.
Russians captured him first, but
he snuck past their guarded gate

with a water pail, crouched for three days
in the dead woods, traded his coat for
a glass of milk before the Nazis came,

stuffed him with the others in a barn loft.
Those who spilled out fell on bayonets.
The lucky ones ate bark and leaves

behind barbed wire. But even the SS needed shoes,
so he signed up to mend soles, tack leather,
earn an extra bowl of hot soup. By war's end,

he came to your town to shovel coal. You knew
he'd never go back. You only wished
to still his trembling hands, keep him warm.

So you took his skinny ring, bribed police
with homemade whiskey, packed it up
for a long boat ride, a better life in New York.

Got by with odd jobs and broken English.
He laid bricks, you cleaned houses.
Seven years it took to build your new home

in Floral Park. Neighbors would stop by
for a round of beer, a shot of schnapps,
polka songs he paid you a quarter *not* to sing.

Check after check he sent to Poland.
You'd scold him for it. He'd give it all away
to save the ones he left behind.

When cancer took root, he swore off doctors.
You'd walk him to the shower, stumble
like drunk lovers in the hallway, collapse

in laughter. The home nurse says you still
talk to Alex as you watch the late-night shows.
He comes in the quiet hours,

asking about the shoe tools
you keep in boxes buried in the garage.
No one knows what to do with them.

Alive

Garage door roars open
to wake the room
that time forgot:

old push mower
with its wobbly wheels,

loppers and slingblade
retired on wall hooks,

axe handle
gnawed like a bone.

Fat spiders dangle
in dark corners.

Something slept here,
slinked away,

left its shape
twined around
a metal grate.

Long as a child's arm,
crinkly as cellophane.

I place it
in the back of my car,
and wonder

on the dusty ride
down the mountain

if this coiled skin will rouse
to become what it was—

twisting, writhing,
licking the air.

II.

*Then said they unto him, Say now Shibboleth: and he said
Sibboleth: for he could not frame to pronounce it right. Then they took
him, and slew him at the passages of Jordan: and there fell at that time of
the Ephraimites forty and two thousand.*

— Judges 12:6

Shibboleth

In the days of Gilead when tribe fought tribe
for fat cattle and a place at the well,
knowing *how* to say the name of a town
meant more than oasis, meant you were welcome,
and they wouldn't have to slit your throat
or burn your tent in the middle of the night.
So before you go embarrassing yourself,
mangling the names of crossroads and rivers,
remember the subtle ways of those who know
where you're from by the way you speak—
who you are, where you're headed.
Folks you mistake for slow have a quick ear
to tell the difference between native
and stranger, neighbor and trespasser.
Before you come to claim your acre
where cemeteries mark centuries
and the past is always present,
ease your tongue into the right accent,
carry pronunciation like a passport.
No need to tell your life story.
When the time comes to speak,
listen. Learn the lay of language.
Here, these words become your home,
or leave you wishing it was.

Yay-long

It is most certainly not a member of the metric system,
perhaps a distant relation to the foot or yard.

Snubbed by the methodical and meticulous
who pride themselves with empirical accuracy,

it endures as a standard among Southerners
when a tape measure won't do.

How big was that possum? the man at the gas station asks.
'Bout yay-long, his friend replies, hands spread wide, like so.

Yay-long or yay-high declares without stretching
the truth to eleventy feet. Used sparingly,

yay-long lends credibility to the speaker,
unlike its coarse cousin, *big-ass.*

Yay-long approximates for those who didn't see
the neighbor's copperhead startled in the wood pile.

A breath of anticipation between those hands,
experience borne from the invisible.

Yay-long serves memory as memory serves the teller,
and so we nod, eager for the rest of the story.

Toothjumping

A remedy once
for tinking loose an achy tooth
with hammer and chisel—
tools from a trusted neighbor
who came to solve
the riddle of jaw splinter.

A shot of whiskey, a steady chair,
and a word of warning:
one false tap, one slight twitch
and teeth might spray
like ice chips or worse—
bloody scream, cracked smile
to wear till the end of your days.

But if metal struck true,
that irksome incisor,
that galling gum-throbber,
that vexatious vittle-chomper,
popped right out like a seed
spit from watermelon.

Shine

In the back of beyond where
streams ran pure and the still stayed
hidden from meddling neighbors
and federal agents, hard men
stood guard over coils and pots,
sheet metal and copper pipes,
homemade brews of corn and rye,
thirst and fire. Bottled in barns
for late night deliveries,
mountain dew came to dry towns
on jacked-up trucks, haul-ass tires.
Cash money at the back door.
Corn liquor settled old debts,
torched a cough, bought shoes and coats
for the little ones. One swig
from a Mason jar and you'd
know why they called it pop-skull,
wobble water, white lightning.
Nowadays, the tourist towns
sell it like soda, legal
as lemonade. Triple X
on the merchandise. T-shirts
and billboard signs summon all
the corny caricatures—
bucktoothed John in overalls,
Jenny Mae in Daisy Dukes,
dueling banjos, grinning bears,
country cabins spelled with K's.
At the next intersection,
the neon flashes *Snake Juice*,
a new brew on the same game—
sweet elixirs from hucksters
out to make a fortune off
a mountain they'd never climb.

The Flood

An army of clouds
crowded the sky.
Winds kicked up,
knocked over ladders,
mailboxes, swingsets,
swept through fields
of unfinished crops.
A chatter of rain,
a busy tapping.
Pellets. Chains.
Sheets of rain.
What the old-timers call
a gullywasher, a sod soaker.
Merciless, unrelenting.
Puddles huddled. Creeks rivered.
Hour after hour, dawn to night,
as if this were all
we would ever know,
a rain to end our days,
a rain that unloosed roots,
choked gutters, poured over floors,
spilled down streets, ripped out
rock walls and chunks of sidewalk,
turned cars into bars of soap.
Seventeen inches, the weatherman said.
And when it was over,
we peeked out of our homes.
An eerie quiet, a sky washed clean.
Some walked to where
the bridge had been.
A mud hungry river raged.
We watched the current
carry away tree branches and
park benches, tin roofs and street signs,
bobbing peppers and tomatoes,
the flotsam of our once familiar world
taken to some giant drain
miles downstream.

The Devil Beats His Wife

Older brothers would sneak up,
cigarette in hand, hold her down
till the shock of heat left its mark.

It was some meanness family made up
to pass the time, she thought, and learned
to sleep with one eye open.

Daddy damn near made her deaf
when a Marlboro got stuck
in her left ear. She was ten.

When she found her baby's first burn,
she waited for Uncle Jay to pass out
on the couch Sunday afternoon, lit

two Salem Lights, crept through
the trailer, fire in her eyes.
He smacked her away screaming.

Outside it was sunny and raining,
the time when folks like to say
the devil beats his wife.

Flesh and Blood

Strung from the rusty halo of a basketball goal,
a deer with a stick between its legs
hangs by a rope. As rain threatens,
the men emerge from a doublewide,
the women a step behind. A toddler peeks out
of a doorway. Pit bull lurches from his chain.
In the neighbor's yard, a boy studies the scene,
replays the hunt with a BB rifle and a fallen bike.
Once again, the men of Sycamore Creek have come
to split shanks under a sheet-metal barn
that sizzles when it rains. They trade tales
about skipping school to cast a line, track a buck—
lost exploits and misadventures in the woods,
that time the treed panther turned out to be
a possum or when a black bear made off with
Uncle Buck's dentures. Between laughs, a hard pause,
almost a prayer, a reprieve from hauling heavy loads,
mending fence posts, tractor debt, twenty years digging
in the earth for a crop that don't pay,
Nana's cancer pills, and soon another mouth to feed.
In the moth-eaten lamplight, they gather around
a blood-stained table. One among them steps forth
with steady hands and hungry blade,
ready to carve the kill.

Bull Elk in Cataloochee

We come in late summer,
pilgrims armed with Canons
and Nikons, drawn to the valley
once home to corn and cattle,
Palmers and Caldwells.
Thief still, we stand watch, waiting
for the flick of a tail, twitch of an ear,
branch of antler among sugar maple.
One by one, hoof and hide emerge
to graze in a sprawling meadow.
Chief among them steps forth,
snorts a musky breath.
For weeks he will forsake food
to herd his white-rumped harem,
ward off rivals with a single cry
that startles the air—
a long shrill note,
ancient, defiant,
a call to all things wild.

Our only reply is silence.

Girl with Guitar, 1947

she'll take your dare
with that spitfire grin
glint of mischief
in glade green eyes

frayed pigtails dangle
like wrestled rope
on a denim shirt
that smells
of honeysuckle

patches on her britches
bare feet dirt-pocked
from chasing cousins
yard to stream

she perches
in a flatback chair
a Martin guitar straddled
between her legs

after supper
family gathers
on the porch

Daddy strums
an old tune
they all know by heart

Mama sings a ballad
of a lonesome love
that ends with a hanging

trees slow their sway
the starry pond shivers

the girl picks up her guitar
ready for a song
she's been waiting
her whole life to play

Infare, 1898

Let us gather at the bend in the river
known as Loving Place.
Let no one put asunder
what these two bind together—
she of the West Fork clan,
he of a Crabtree farm.
Give thanks. I do. Amen.

Then lead us by horse
and wagon up the road
to the groom's farmhouse
where a fat hog awaits
the carving knife. Boil some
taters, a mess of beans.
Biscuits and gravy. Save room
for sweet cream and a cobbler
that bleeds blackberry.

After supper, push back
the chairs and listen to
the Barley boys saw that fiddle—
*Cluck Old Hen, Fox on the Run,
Tennessee Reel.* Pass around
the pertinin' juice, let it light
a fire upon your lips before you
buss a pretty girl's cheek.
Out back, grab the groom,
make him ride a rail.
See if he squirms free.

When the moon hangs low,
the revelers bid farewell.
Hush out the last candle.
Listen to the creek, a light wind
through the wheat fields.

Then comes the clang of tin cans,
jingly bells, pistol fire.
The shindig starts up again.
It's all been done before,
this waking of the newly wed—
just so they know family
is only a holler away.

Home Guard
for Private Elijah Jenkins, Co. E, 29th N.C. Infantry Regiment (1828-1865)

I was the son of rock creeks and dark hollers.
Born to farm the fallow fields, I learned
the promise of yoke and plow, leaned

my back into shallow swaths
of crooked earth, took a wife
who bore me sons to hunt

and shuck. When war came,
I kissed my Polly goodbye, told the boys
to fatten up a hog for my return.

Mama wrapped corn pone and a Bible
in my haversack. We mustered up in Asheville,
swore no army would set foot in these hills.

Haywood Fire Shooters they called us.
Sent those Federals on the run
from Mobile to Cumberland Gap,

whupped ol' Rosy and his boys
at Murfreesboro and Chickamauga,
but damn that General Bragg,

made us turn and run like dogs.
We cursed his name, marched on
half rations through mud and snow.

I prayed for wool socks and a letter
from home, kept my jackknife clean,
stuck a lucky button in my pocket.

When they captured us in Alabama,
I had no shirt, no shoes, no Bible.
Providence spared me a year in prison.

I dreamt of spring rain on a new crop of corn,
hoecakes blessed with apple butter,
smoked bacon spitting on a hickory fire.

I took their Oath, made my way home
to Cove Creek where Polly fell upon me
with sour news. Young Thomas had caught

the fever. Will she buried last winter.
Long nights we lay under her quilts,
a harrying wind at our door.

Come May, I worked a bony mule
in a field of stump and stone, a barn
half built. That's when the Home Guard came,

hot as the devil's whiskey, still waging
their own war, stealing livestock
and whatever else was hid from Union raids.

Said I was a deserter, dragged me
to the woods, bound me like a runaway slave.
We trod by night to White Oak,

where a jury of one-armed men stood
around a campfire. Such crimes as mine
harbor no mercy, and no truth would set me free.

Three days later on a hilltop of sarvis,
friends laid me to rest, far from the cannon
in a country I once called home.

III.

Some stories are true that never happened.

—Elie Wiesel

And every story has a story that hides inside its own labyrinth.

— Malena Mörling

Spearfinger

I could have been someone's granny,
wretched hag in ragged robes,
roaming the woods, looking to cure
an old wound. It wasn't always so.

Hungry as a child, I ran to the creek
to steal the plumpest berries I'd ever seen.
That's where the witches found me,
bound me with nettles,

bade me drink their bitter wine.
Under a blood moon they danced
around a queer fire, chanting
their spell to change me.

Tickseed, chestnut, twisted stalks.
By these leaves, know our thoughts.
Bugbane, bloodroot, bergamot wild.
Take this, make this, Spearfinger child.

Wizened and wooly-haired
I woke to do their bidding:
called out to a curious child,
coaxed her onto my lap, brushed her hair.

One long, bony finger would rise
from my curséd hand, stab quick
like an awl through a toad's belly
to filch a liver. No scar, no blood.

Only the vague ache of slow death.
Before you knew it, I would be
in your home looking like an old maid
who went out for a morning walk

and came back sooner than expected.
Half a village would fall ill,
poison spilling through their veins.
Pale skin, hung jaw, the stony stare.

I carried their livers back to the witches
who dined on raw meat and foul drink.
Turn me back! I cried.
Cackle and hiss, their only reply.

I had no hunger for this world.
Into the fog I ran through laurel hells
and hardscrabble until each step became
another stone I could not carry.

Tickseed, chestnut, twisted stalks.
By these leaves, know my thoughts.
Bugbane, bloodroot, bergamot wild.
Heed me, leave me, Spearfinger child.

Weary and numb, I stumbled,
fell deep into a hunter's pit,
dug to snare the thing I'd become.
Pierce her heart! the village men yelled.

But their sharpest spears broke upon
stone-hard skin. I had taken a new form,
taller and stronger than any man alive,
a statue rising from hollowed ground.

That's when the luckiest of arrows
pierced the palm of my hand,
where the witches had hidden my power.
I began to bleed. The wicked finger shattered.

Stone upon stone crumbled into avalanche
until all the men would find the next day
was a mound of rocks covering
a little girl lost in the woods.

Uk'tena

When the sun with its cruel rays
sent a fever among the Cherokee,
the medicine men summoned
a great serpent to swallow the sun,
but the beast failed, fell upon
smoky mountains, took refuge in the wild
where brave men dared not speak its name.
Elders claimed its weight crushed rock,
curved rivers. Its diamond forehead
blinded those who sought to snare it.
Beware the fangs, long as spears,
antlers too. Each tale of its sighting
added menace to myth.
In the summer of '76, it woke
to the smell of blood and fire,
Redcoat and Patriot.
From the East it came
over Swannanoa Gap,
across the French Broad,
its long, scaly tail glinting
like a thousand flintlocks.
Fiery venom cut a trace through cane
and thornstalk, along the banks
of Hominy Creek, over Pigeon
and Tuckasegee rivers. It struck
the towns of the *Tsa-lagi*,
flattened cornfields, slaughtered cattle,
scorched houses, sent mothers running
a mad path up Cowee Mountain
until the beast chanced upon
the setting sun, that foe of old.
Down a rock chasm it chased
the last embers of day, swallowed hard
in the raging waters of the Nantahala.
Some say when the moon wanes
and men dream of war, you can feel
the pull of a long shadow across cliff walls
as the sun fades and the earth trembles.

Beasts of Eden

Perhaps they grew tired
of dew-golden grasses,
the sleepy haze of eternal sun,
endless rehearsals of harp song.

Perhaps they ambled too close
to the forbidden tree, tasted
its bitter fruit, nibbled seeds
the serpent left behind.

Was it their wish to follow the path
of the only man they ever knew?
Or did they ache as Eve did to touch
the threads of a retreating horizon?

And if they could leave, did they
venture out on their own accord,
noses nudging gates left ajar,
a steady exodus of herds and flocks?

None can say if they ever returned,
for the garden lies hidden by a border
vague as fog, steep as silence,
a mist between worlds.

Perhaps to this day, the angels still
let slip a few of God's oldest designs,
curious beasts with furious beauty,
the first and last of their kind.

David

One rock from the River Jordan
borne from mud, a baby's fist.

He tosses it a few times,
lets it drop in his palm

as if to lessen its weight
before loading a borrowed slingshot.

The crowd leans toward
this chosen one called to slay.

Each side bangs shields, raises
swords, screams insults of victory.

Too many voices to hear just one.
Then Goliath appears,

his thick arms scarred from battle,
sword scabbed with rusty flesh.

The boy steps forth trembling,
fingers numb, heart a tambourine.

There can be no second shot,
only this one, guided by faith,

aimed at the giant's forehead,
a temple doomed to spill

its ruby secrets. Two armies inhale
as a stone hisses through sandy air.

Milk and Honey

God was sick of the children of Israel
whining in the desert. It was summer
in the Book of Numbers—a long ride
to the nearest Shell station.
Moab could have been Timbuktu
for all they cared. Even the manna
had gotten stale. Down to hummus
and baked chips, they were tired of
schlepping tents, digging for water
in all the wrong places. Just once,
it'd be nice to sit poolside in Palm Beach
with Lox and a bagel, fresh OJ
and a *Times* crossword.
                              Moses,
newly diagnosed with colon cancer,
knew he wouldn't set foot in Canaan.
If only his people could catch a glimpse
of those green pastures the TV ads promised.
Maybe then it would all be worth it—
Yul Brenner's scowls, the endless plagues,
sandstorms and bickering tribes,
waking from nightmares where chariots
chased them over cliffs and golden calves
swallowed their children.

Miles from the nearest miracle,
Moses would rise before dawn,
hike alone in the hills beyond camp,
recall his mother's knishes,
the warm smells of a kosher deli,
the bakery just around the corner
that served the best cheese blintzes,
so tender, so divine.

Samson

Get a load of this barbell-bending biceptual.
Studmeister with the six-pack
and bench-pressing ritual.
Pec-shaker, jaw-breaker.
Big guns, tight buns.
Watch this Hebrew Hercules
bring armies to their knees.
Mystery man of Viagra and Vitalis,
carb-loading cousin of Apollo and Atlas.
Drives around in a top-down Mercedes,
picks up hordes of adoring ladies,
Remember that beguiler Delilah?
Honey-lipped mistress, sumptuous seductress,
cocoa-cream skin, sickle-sharp grin.
Maybe those cinnamon sunrise eyes
caught ol' Sam by surprise.
One night after wrestling in the sheets,
she asked her man, caressing his feet,
What's the secret to your power?
Rare herb or sacred flower?
Tell me, Loverboy, how you came to be
the mightiest man in the Middle E.
The brute blushed, cheeks flushed
from Lady Lilah's sweet entreat.
Babe, he said, *you're misinformed.*
I've been this way since I was born.
No special trick for how it works.
I beat up Philistines and Stone Age jerks.
Now hand me that Gillette, my lil' pet.
Gimme a close shave in this here man-cave.
While you're at it, clip off my dreads
I dig that hipster look instead.
I'm all yours, Dee, can't you see?
Just don't let that razor nick me.
As he kissed her, she whispered,
Sam, my dear, you have nothing to fear.

In God We rust

Someone's lost his faith
under a bridge on I-40.

How else to explain
the missing "T" from gospel graffiti?

On this road to Emmaus,
what are we to believe

when letters writ for
the doubting masses

go missing?
Could it be

the work of atheists
bent on public jest?

A new vision of Hell?
God's withdrawal

from a planet
set on simmer?

Maybe the Man Upstairs
wants us to keep guessing.

Take, for instance,
the dove-white church van

stalled in rush-hour traffic
proclaiming with its bumper sticker

Paradise Falls.

Sisyphus in the Parking Lot

Welcome to Hell—
where the customers arrive

ready to buy whatever
the jingly ads have promised—

everlasting youth, instant euphoria,
customized comfort, satisfaction guaranteed.

Modern convenience brought to us by
the discount kings of frozen pizza,

plastic furniture, handguns
laxatives, hair gel, ice cream.

Charge it all to the cards
that keep us in debt for eternity.

And once we've stuffed our cars
with gut gloss and wonder wax,

wart removers and dirt dissolvers
mood rings and chicken wings,

there's a young man
willing to take our carts.

We've seen him a million times
though we never think to ask for his name—

lanky teen in khakis and a button-up shirt,
bright orange safety vest.

Too shy to speak, too tired for words,
he toils weekends and school nights,

saving up for a car he can't afford,
but he takes pride being the one

to track down all those stray carts
shoved in corrals, ditched along curbs,

stranded like cars in a snowstorm.
He is their shepherd, their conductor,

fitting them together in a long,
unwieldy train that clatters back

to the station, only to watch them escape
again and again, hour after hour,

because the customers keep coming
and this store never closes.

The Golden Cup

It had been years since Midas rid himself
of the wish that turned flesh

to precious metal—his only daughter
silenced into statuary. Still married

to his penance, the king sought daily
the queen's forgiveness, scrubbed his hands

with harsh soaps and oily salves, never sure
his fingers would be cured of the poison.

He buried his crown, banned coins
from court, sent alms to the poor.

Those closest to his touch dared not
speak of the days he nearly went mad.

So imagine the gasps when a gaunt man
from a faraway land stood before the king

bearing a golden cup. Imagine the swift sentence
for such a crime. Advisors spurned the fool

and his brazen gift, but Midas bid him
come forward, speak his mind.

You are too kind, the stranger said, *I only ask
that you drink but once from this cup*

*to lift my curse. Surely you know
the gods who sent me. I carry a thirst*

*not of this world.
I am Tantalus.*

Pills for Pygmalion

Years after Venus turned chiseled art
into supple skin, cold stone to warm hips,
the famed artist now finds himself reaching
for the hand of his immortal love—
if only he could recall her name.
The stroke last month left his right side limp,
his eyes hazy. He sleeps most days,
mistakes the remote for a hairbrush,
mumbles about the phone he hears ringing.
She brings him TV dinners and chocolate bars,
doles out the meds, empties the bed pan.
Some days he remembers what it was like
after he took her off that pedestal, showed her
his world—summers in Santorini, sailing to Crete,
nights of wine and poetry, mornings among
hyacinths, loaves and goat cheese at the market.
Tonight, she grinds an extra dose of powder
into his tea, strokes his cheek, hums a melody
they once sang togther. Soon he will be free.
Soon the marble gods will have their sculptor.

Trace

If we are taught to parse time
into nanoseconds, spot blips of ships
on radar, mark the start of the cosmos
with quarks, then surely dominions
of minutiae deserve their own monument
worthy of veneration. Bring forth
marble to carve their names—
    Iota   *Trivia*   *Miniscule.*
For they are the microns and milligrams
that nudge us toward victory or catastrophe.
Let beggar and general pay tribute
to these smidgeoneers or suffer
the blinding flash of their alchemy.
Mere mites they are, borne on the whims
of the wind, until they take hold, congregate,
slip through a cell wall, dance too close
to an electron and va-whoosh!
A chain reaction, an avalanche.
One bit more, one speck less
turns crack to chasm, pox to pandemic,
star to smithereens.

Mad Scientist

Give me an underground laboratory, half a dozen atom-smashers, and a beautiful girl in a diaphanous veil waiting to be turned into a chimpanzee, and I care not who writes the nation's laws.
— S.J. Perelman

He's at it again with those bubbling vats,
cooking up some secret experiment
where impending disaster awaits.
On the verge of greatness, his contraptions
never seem to work, those loopy tubes
and fizzy potions ready for another explosion.
The world needs his genius, he tells himself.
He will not be deterred when rivals steal
his equations, when green vapors singe his skin,
when lab rats escape before he can inject them
with a serum for super-human strength.
The boys at school left him with this limp.
Neighbors ignored his enigmatic rants,
so he went underground, found a black market
that killed to have his expertise, gave him
plenty of live subjects and a huge lab
with steel chambers where he could invent
his own science, spin dark matter into
infinite energy. Let them scoff. Let them wonder
what he's up to. Soon their sneers will become
his delight, a quick snicker erupting into
deep bellows that echo through tunnels
under this sleeping city. Soon the world
will marvel at this goggle-eyed man
one ion shy of a power no one will tame.

Superman's Laundry

Whatever happened to all those suits
Clark Kent left in phone booths?

Did they disintegrate in a whirling blur
just before flight? Or did they fall

into a crumpled pile
hidden like his identity?

Surely, Superman came back after catching
a plunging plane with his bare hands,

and gathered his pants,
shirt, tie, jacket, and shoes—

unless someone else beat him to it,
made off with a little pocket change,

a few pens from *The Daily Planet*. Perhaps
the Man of Steel meant to leave it all behind.

Imagine, while saving Metropolis,
he was giving away clothes to the homeless.

And what of his costume, the smog-worn cape?
Having battled apocalyptic aliens

from another dimension, where did Superman go
to shower off the grease, the villainous slime?

Batman had Alfred to polish boots and belts.
For Spider-Man, Aunt May offered a hot bath.

But where was Superman's front-load washer?
How do you scrub away stains that stick like kryptonite?

How do you cheer for a superhero
if you can't read the "S" on his chest?

Problems with Flight

If you have not yet flown on a magic carpet, you probably don't know about the seasickness.
— Salmon Rushdie, Luka and the Fire of Life

You'd be surprised by what gets stuck
in fairy wings—
sand   bugs   sap   gum,
flecks of old paint,
plastic bags that would swallow you whole.

Capes flap in your face,
tear at the neckline,
tangle in the splintered metal
of runaway trains.

Brooms don't come with saddles.
Long rides incur bruising, chafing,
numbness in the nether regions.
And contrary to popular belief,
black cats are reluctant travellers.

They don't tell you it gets lonely up there.

Sure, there's a great view.
Nothing like a mile-high sunrise
or that swell of sea as you race across waves.
The queasy hesitations
over heights and deathly plunges
eventually subside.

Of course, traveling at ethereal speeds
doesn't mean you're immune to collisions
with birds, trees, jet engines,
sudden hailstorms.

Like all good stories that begin
with the best of intentions,
even magic carpets
have threads that unravel.

Endnotes

• "Girl with Guitar, 1947" — This poem refers to a photograph by W. Eugene Smith that was part of a photographic essay titled "Folk Singers." It was taken during a folk festival Smith attended in Asheville, N.C. – mostly likely the Mountain Dance and Folk Festival.

• "Infare, 1898" — An infare, once a common Southern Appalachian tradition, was a dinner and reception following a wedding, usually held at the home of the groom or the groom's parents with festive music, dancing and games. After the party was over and the newlyweds were alone, the family would return in the middle of the night for another round of loud carousing that could include pistol fire, pots and pans clanging, and all sorts of noise.

• "Home Guard" — This poem imagines a background story for Elijah Jenkins, a Confederate soldier from Haywood County in western North Carolina who was captured, imprisoned and later released at the end of the Civil War, only to be captured and killed by the Home Guard.

• "Spearfinger" — This poem is based on the Cherokee legend of Spearfinger, a shapeshifting ogress who often took the form of a grandmother and who used her spearlike finger to steal the livers of children. With her powers of stealth, skin of stone, and a heart secretly hidden in her hand, she was almost impossible to kill. This poem invents an alternative narrative about how she came to be and how she was captured.

• "Ut'kena" — This mythical Cherokee serpent had huge features, including massive fangs, antlers and a powerful diadem on its forehead that could turn a person to stone or ruin if you laid eyes on it. This poem also illustrates a terrible historical episode in the fall of 1776 when American colonists marched into western North Carolina to destroy Cherokee towns that were rumored to be allied with the British during the Revolutionary War.

Acknowledgments

Many thanks for the generous support from poet friends who saw various versions of these poems in workshops and critique groups, including the Bard Owl Poets and Marathon Poets. Thanks especially for the honest advice and encouragement from poets Cathy Smith Bowers, Susan Lefler, Michael McFee and Fred Chappell, who continue to inspire me to write the poems I've been meaning to write. I am also grateful for the wisdom and guidance from Kathryn Stripling Byer and Susan Laughter Meyers. So blessed for the friends I've met and insights I've gained from the Great Smokies Writing Program at UNC-Asheville, the Appalachian Writers Workshop at Hindman, Ky.; Wildacres Retreat in Little Switzerland, N.C.; Press 53's Gathering of Poets in Winston-Salem, N.C., the N.C. Poetry Society, and the Weymouth Center in Southern Pines, N.C. Lastly, a big thanks to Kevin Morgan Watson and Press 53 for turning this manuscipt into a reality.

Michael Beadle is the author of four poetry chapbooks, a poetry CD, and three books on historic photographs of Haywood County in western North Carolina. His poetry has been published in various journals and anthologies such as *The New Southerner*, *Sow's Ear*, *Great Smokies Review*, and *Kakalak*. His latest chapbook, *Primer* (Main Street Rag, 2017), was a finalist in the 2016 Cathy Smith Bowers Chapbook Contest. In 2012, Michael was selected as a poet-in-residence at the North Carolina Zoo. For the past several years, Michael has been an emcee for the N.C. Poetry Out Loud state finals and served as statewide coordinator of student poetry contests for the NC Poetry Society. For nearly 20 years, he's performed original, contemporary, and classical poetry in schools, festivals, libraries, churches and other venues. As a touring writer-in-residence, he teaches creative writing workshops for students and teachers throughout North Carolina, including the Duke Young Writers' Camp at Duke University. An A+ Schools Fellow since 1999, Michael has taught dozens of arts integration workshops in North Carolina, as well as Michigan, Oklahoma and Iowa.

Cover artist Dawn Surratt studied art at the University of North Carolina at Greensboro as a recipient of the Spencer Love Scholarship in Fine Art. She has exhibited her work throughout the Southeast and currently works as a freelance designer and artist. Her work has been published internationally in magazines, on book covers, and in print media. She lives on the beautiful Kerr Lake in northern North Carolina with her husband, one demanding cat, and a crazy Pembroke Welsh Corgi.

www.ingramcontent.com/pod-product-compliance
Lightning Source LLC
LaVergne TN
LVHW041346080426
835512LV00006B/639